FRIENDSHIP

FRIENDSHIP

Biblical TRUTHS

— *that* —

Bring Us Together

B&H
PUBLISHING GROUP

NASHVILLE, TENNESSEE

Published by B&H Publishing Group
Nashville, Tennessee

Dewey Decimal Classification: 242.5
Subject Heading: DEVOTIONAL LITERATURE \
BIBLE—INSPIRATION \ MEDITATIONS \ PRAYERS

1 2 3 4 5 6 7 8 • 22 21 20 19 18

CONTENTS

CONTENTS

Somewhere along the line, the Bible attracted a reputation for being both irrelevant and impossible to understand. Out of touch as well as out of reach. Yet while conclusions like these continue to persist, so does human need for the Bible to be everything God affirms it to be: "living and effective" (Hebrews 4:12), its message "very near you, in your mouth and in your heart" (Deuteronomy 30:14).

If families and friends are to live together in unity . . . if lives are to be whole and fruitful in heart and mind . . . if tragedy and loss and disappointment and confusion are to be survived . . . no, not merely survived but transformed into peace and power and a purposeful way forward . . . you need a Word that is here and now and able to be grasped. You need to "know the truth," because "the truth will set you free" (John 8:32).

You need to take a step back and soak in God's Word.

Filled with Scriptures that speak personally to you this little book is further proof that God intends His Word to share living space with your present reality. Always in touch. Always within reach. No matter where you are, or what you are going through, allow this book to help direct you to the Scriptures you need most.

An unkind word, a missed dinner, a forgotten birthday. There are countless occasions in every friendship for anger to rear its ugly head. It's an emotion that we all feel, and tend to feel, the most often toward those we care about the most. The key is not to act out in anger, but remember the value of the friendship and no matter what the cause of the anger, to always speak and act with love.

*Refrain from anger and give up your rage; do not be
agitated—it can only bring harm.*

   Psalm 37:8

———

*A patient person shows great understanding, but a
quick-tempered one promotes foolishness.*

   Proverbs 14:29

———

*A gentle answer turns away anger, but a harsh word
stirs up wrath.*

   Proverbs 15:1

"*But I tell you, everyone who is angry with his brother or sister will be subject to judgment. Whoever insults his brother or sister, will be subject to the court. Whoever says, 'You fool!' will be subject to hellfire.*"
    Matthew 5:22

———

Be angry and do not sin. Don't let the sun go down on your anger, and don't give the devil an opportunity.
    Ephesians 4:26–27

Lord, thank You for the friendships You have placed in my life. Right now I am holding on to anger in my heart. Wipe this anger out of me. Give me the peace and patience that I need to forgive my friend. Remind me daily of the forgiveness that You have given me. I desire to love and serve them well, but I know I cannot do this without Your guiding hand. Grant me the wisdom to know how to handle this situation in love. Amen

Anxiety can come up in every part of our lives. Beneath our anxieties is a need to feel in control. Control in any relationship is impossible. It is about give and take and releasing your control in exchange for relationship. Our peace is found in knowing that the Creator of the universe holds us safely in the palm of His hand and will protect us no matter the situation in which we land.

"Therefore I tell you: Don't worry about your life, what you will eat or what you will drink; or about your body, what you will wear. Isn't life more than food and the body more than clothing? Consider the birds of the sky: They don't sow or reap or gather into barns, yet your heavenly Father feeds them. Aren't you worth more than they? Can any of you add one moment to his life-span by worrying?"

    Matthew 6:25–27

———

Don't worry about anything, but in everything, through prayer and petition with thanksgiving, present your requests to God. And the peace of God, which surpasses all understanding, will guard your hearts and minds in Christ Jesus.

    Philippians 4:6–7

"Peace I leave with you. My peace I give to you. I do not give to you as the world gives. Don't let your heart be troubled or fearful."

    John 14:27

———

For God has not given us a spirit of fear, but one of power, love, and sound judgment.

    2 Timothy 1:7

———

Humble yourselves, therefore, under the mighty hand of God, so that he may exalt you at the proper time, casting all your cares on him, because he cares about you.

    1 Peter 5:6–7

Heavenly Father, sometimes I feel anxiety in my friendships. I worry that I am not doing enough, or too much, or am not fully known or fully loved. Even though I know that I cannot hold the reins in a relationship, I still feel lost without some kind of control. Help me to leave my anxieties at Your feet. I entrust to You my friendships, knowing that Your peace will guard my heart and mind. Amen

Friendships play an important role in our lives. They give us strength when we need it most. Friendships do not just appear out of nowhere. They are like flowers in a garden that must be cared for. Today, look for ways that you can show your friends that you care about them. Think about the ways in which your friends show their care for you.

*"I give you a new command: Love one another.
Just as I have loved you, you are also to love one
another. By this everyone will know that you are my
disciples, if you love one another."*
    John 13:34–35

———

*Carry one another's burdens; in this way you will
fulfill the law of Christ.*
    Galatians 6:2

Therefore, as we have opportunity, let us work for the good of all, especially for those who belong to the household of faith.

Galatians 6:10

———

Everyone should look out not only for his own interests, but also for the interests of others.

Philippians 2:4

Father God, help me reflect Your gracious patience and unfailing love. Show me ways to love and care for my friends well. It is so easy for me to take my relationships for granted and forget that if they are neglected they could easily disappear. Show me ways today that I can show my friends how much I care for them. Help me to see the ways in which they care for me, and let me not ever take for granted having them in my life. Amen

None of us are immune from hardships, loss, and grief, but we can take heart that no matter what has happened, the Lord promises to comfort us. Sometimes He comforts us directly, sometimes through circumstances, and sometimes through the people He places in our lives. Think about the ways that God has comforted you in your times of need.

Even when I go through the darkest valley, I fear no danger, for you are with me; your rod and your staff—they comfort me.

Psalm 23:4

———

Remember your word to your servant; you have given me hope through it. This is my comfort in my affliction: Your promise has given me life.

Psalm 119:49–50

———

As a mother comforts her son, so I will comfort you, and you will be comforted in Jerusalem.

Isaiah 66:13

"Blessed are those who mourn, for they will be comforted."
  Matthew 5:4

———

Blessed be the God and Father of our Lord Jesus Christ, the Father of mercies and the God of all comfort. He comforts us in all our affliction, so that we may be able to comfort those who are in any kind of affliction, through the comfort we ourselves receive from God.
  2 Corinthians 1:3–4

Dear God, thank You for comforting me and healing my heart in times of trial. Thank You for putting people in my life who bring me comfort. Guide me to those whom You have chosen for me as kindred spirits. Guide my actions that I may be a source of comfort for others. Use my life as a blessing for others. Amen

The Lord commands us to love our neighbors as ourselves and to also love our enemies—godly compassion is speaking and acting out of love in the best interests of others. Just like you would be willing to drop everything to help your dearest friend, you should be just as willing to have compassion for a stranger. This level of compassion is not possible on your own, and is only possible through the Holy Spirit inside of you.

Yet he was compassionate; he atoned for their iniquity and did not destroy them. He often turned his anger aside and did not unleash all his wrath.

    Psalm 78:38

———

When he went ashore, he saw a large crowd and had compassion on them, because they were like sheep without a shepherd. Then he began to teach them many things.

    Mark 6:34

*Carry one another's burdens; in this way you will
fulfill the law of Christ.*

Galatians 6:2

———

*And be kind and compassionate to one another,
forgiving one another, just as God also forgave you
in Christ.*

Ephesians 4:32

Lord, may Your Holy Spirit fill my heart and soul with concern for my family, friends, neighbors, colleagues, and even enemies. Father, sometimes it is difficult for me to have compassion on those I consider deserving of their grief. Remove this hate from within me. Help me to see people the way You see them, and not through my own weaknesses. Open up my heart to the people around me that I may be a willing conduit of Your love. Amen

The longer you have been in any kind of
relationship with someone, the more likely the
chance that you have already experienced some
kind of conflict with them. Conflict can arise
from any number of situations from pride,
jealousy, misunderstanding, shame, or even
just ignorance. One way we can walk in the
Spirit, rather than according to the flesh, is to
resist the pride and need to be right that we
often feel in conflicts with others.

*Therefore, putting away lying, speak the truth, each
one to his neighbor, because we are members of one
another. Be angry and do not sin. Don't let the sun
go down on your anger, and don't give the devil an
opportunity.*

  Ephesians 4:25–27

———

*Bless those who persecute you; bless and do not
curse. Rejoice with those who rejoice; weep with
those who weep. Live in harmony with one another.
Do not be proud; instead, associate with the humble.
Do not be wise in your own estimation. Do not repay
anyone evil for evil. Give careful thought to do what
is honorable in everyone's eyes. If possible, as far as
it depends on you, live at peace with everyone.*

  Romans 12:14–18

What is the source of wars and fights among you?
Don't they come from your passions that wage
war within you? You desire and do not have. You
murder and covet and cannot obtain. You fight and
wage war. You do not have because you do not ask.

    James 4:1–2

———

"If your brother sins against you, go and rebuke
him in private. If he listens to you, you have won
your brother. But if he won't listen, take one or two
others with you, so that by the testimony of two or
three witnesses every fact may be established. If he
doesn't pay attention to them, tell the church. If he
doesn't pay attention even to the church, let him be
like a Gentile and a tax collector to you."

    Matthew 18:15–17

Lord Jesus, my heart is full of conflict and resentment. Even after I claim to have forgiven my friends I still hold on to the hurt and allow it to push me away from trust and into the throws of conflict. God, give me patience and peace. May I imitate Your grace and gentleness in every disagreement or confrontation with people in my life. Amen

At home, at work, in friendships, in families, in life—contentment is hard! We are constantly looking around to see what could be better or what we are missing out on. The quickest route to contentment is through gratitude and trust; gratitude to God for what He has provided you and trust that He will continue to give you everything you need. Recognize the abundant goodness in your life. See the good, and trust that God never fails to provide for your needs.

*"So don't worry, saying, 'What will we eat?' or
'What will we drink?' or 'What will we wear?'
For the Gentiles eagerly seek all these things,
and your heavenly Father knows that you need
them. But seek first the kingdom of God and his
righteousness, and all these things will be provided
for you. Therefore don't worry about tomorrow,
because tomorrow will worry about itself. Each day
has enough trouble of its own."*

Matthew 6:31–34

———

*He then told them, "Watch out and be on guard
against all greed, because one's life is not in the
abundance of his possessions."*

Luke 12:15

I don't say this out of need, for I have learned to be content in whatever circumstances I find myself. I know both how to make do with little, and I know how to make do with a lot. In any and all circumstances I have learned the secret of being content—whether well fed or hungry, whether in abundance or in need.

    Philippians 4:11–12

———

But godliness with contentment is great gain. For we brought nothing into the world, and we can take nothing out. If we have food and clothing, we will be content with these.

    1 Timothy 6:6–8

Heavenly Father, thank You for Your unfailing love and faithfulness. Father, when I am lost in discontentment, push me to see all that You have provided for me. Do not allow me to continue to be blind, but open my eyes to the goodness that surrounds me exactly where I am. Grow in me a godly contentment, never wishing I was anywhere but exactly where You have placed me. Amen

Where do you find your delight? Is it in your family? Your job? Your accomplishments? Your nights out with your friends? Your hobbies? What is it that makes your heart sing? Without Christ our delight is only in our own sinful desires, but once we have the Holy Spirit within us, we no longer delight in the things of this world. We delight in the Lord, and in His desires. We even delight in His instruction because we know that it is for our good.

How happy is the one who does not walk in the advice of the wicked or stand in the pathway with sinners or sit in the company of mockers! Instead, his delight is in the LORD's instruction, and he meditates on it day and night. He is like a tree planted beside flowing streams that bears its fruit in its season and whose leaf does not wither. Whatever he does prospers.

Psalm 1:1–3

———

The LORD your God is among you, a warrior who saves. He will rejoice over you with gladness. He will be quiet in his love. He will delight in you with singing.

Zephaniah 3:17

He brought me out to a spacious place; he rescued me because he delighted in me.
Psalm 18:19

———

Take delight in the Lord *and he will give you your heart's desires.*
Psalm 37:4

———

If your instruction had not been my delight, I would have died in my affliction. I will never forget your precepts, for you have given me life through them.
Psalm 119:92–93

Father, search my heart and clear away the darkness. If there is any delight in me left for selfish desires, rip it out. Place me in delight for Your instruction, Your creation, and Your glory. Thank You for placing people in my life who I can come together with to delight in You. Amen

A friendship cannot be developed if you only speak to each other once a year. It takes time, commitment, and devotion to the relationship. It is the same way with our relationships with God. We cannot show up at church on Sundays and expect that will be enough to have a friendship with Jesus. If you truly care about someone, you desire to spend time with them, to learn them, to know their heart. As you read these verses let them lead you into communion with the Father. Use them as a jumping off point for a life of devotion to Him.

This book of instruction must not depart from your mouth; you are to meditate on it day and night so that you may carefully observe everything written in it. For then you will prosper and succeed in whatever you do.

Joshua 1:8

———

"For where your treasure is, there your heart will be also."

Luke 12:34

"No servant can serve two masters, since either he will hate one and love the other, or he will be devoted to one and despise the other. You cannot serve both God and money."

Luke 16:13

———

Be diligent to present yourself to God as one approved, a worker who doesn't need to be ashamed, correctly teaching the word of truth.

2 Timothy 2:15

Heavenly Father, I know that I do not spend as much time with You as I desire to. I allow my time to disappear as I spend it on the temporary while avoiding the eternal. Convict my heart and make me see my need for devoted time with You. Help me to set aside all distractions and listen to what You have to tell me. Amen

Sometimes the right and wrong answers are easy to see. Should I kill someone? No. Should I read my Bible? Yes. But other times the answers are not as clear. Should I complain to my friend about how difficult my day was? Where should I go to make new friends? Which church should I join? Luckily, these are not decisions you have to make on your own. The Holy Spirit is our ever-present Helper who grants us wisdom so that we can know and do the will of God in all situations.

*So give your servant a receptive heart to judge your
people and to discern between good and evil. For
who is able to judge this great people of yours?*

    1 Kings 3:9

———

*Now if any of you lacks wisdom, he should
ask God—who gives to all generously and
ungrudgingly—and it will be given to him.*

    James 1:5

———

*Don't stifle the Spirit. Don't despise prophecies,
but test all things. Hold on to what is good. Stay
away from every kind of evil.*

    1 Thessalonians 5:19–22

And I pray this: that your love will keep on growing in knowledge and every kind of discernment, so that you may approve the things that are superior and may be pure and blameless in the day of Christ.
    Philippians 1:9–10

———

Dear friends, do not believe every spirit, but test the spirits to see if they are from God, because many false prophets have gone out into the world.
    1 John 4:1

Holy Spirit, may my spirit be open and receptive to Your prompting and leading so that I discern what is right and good in all things. Let my discernment be so strong that I can hear You calling out the directions long before I am led astray. Place in me a heart that sees truth. Amen

God places people in our lives for a reason and for our good. Seek out those who bring you encouragement. Pray for those you can bring encouragement to. Never hold in kindness that can be spread to lift up those around you. You never know when those words are God pouring out encouragement through you to others.

The LORD is the one who will go before you. He will be with you; he will not leave you or abandon you. Do not be afraid or discouraged.

   Deuteronomy 31:8

———

God is our refuge and strength, a helper who is always found in times of trouble.

   Psalm 46:1

———

"Aren't five sparrows sold for two pennies? Yet not one of them is forgotten in God's sight. Indeed, the hairs of your head are all counted. Don't be afraid; you are worth more than many sparrows."

   Luke 12:6–7

"I have told you these things so that in me you may have peace. You will have suffering in this world. Be courageous! I have conquered the world."

 John 16:33

———

And let us watch out for one another to provoke love and good works, not neglecting to gather together, as some are in the habit of doing, but encouraging each other, and all the more as you see the day approaching.

 Hebrews 10:24–25

Christ Jesus, may Your Spirit strengthen and encourage my heart today. Comfort me in my grief, and lift me out of my discouraged state. Show me those around me who need my encouragement. Place on my heart those friends who need a kind word today. Allow me to be the tool You use to help lift up everyone I meet today. Amen

Constantly busy with work, children, school, and family obligations, fellowship with friends and fellow believers can be a difficult thing to find time for. When you do not intentionally schedule it into your week, it can become a thing of the past. But it is important to refresh your heart and soul. Find time this week to be around friends, not as an obligation or with any agenda, but just to fill your cup.

Iron sharpens iron, and one person sharpens another.

    Proverbs 27:17

———

Two are better than one because they have a good reward for their efforts. For if either falls, his companion can lift him up; but pity the one who falls without another to lift him up.

    Ecclesiastes 4:9–10

———

Carry one another's burdens; in this way you will fulfill the law of Christ.

    Galatians 6:2

Therefore encourage one another and build each other up as you are already doing.

    1 Thessalonians 5:11

———

And let us watch out for one another to provoke love and good works, not neglecting to gather together, as some are in the habit of doing, but encouraging each other, and all the more as you see the day approaching.

    Hebrews 10:24–25

Dear Jesus, my heavenly Friend, please reveal to me ways I can spend more time in fellowship and build up others in my community. Show me the times in my schedule where I need to create margin to spend with the people who refresh my soul. Allow my presence to be a blessing to others. Amen

Forgiving someone who has hurt you means you no longer call to mind their fault or error—this extends grace to them and freedom for you. But it is not something that comes naturally, or easily; especially when the hurt has been caused by someone you trusted. This level of forgiveness is only possible by leaning on the Holy Spirit within you, and allowing Him to take control of cleaning your heart.

Therefore I tell you, her many sins have been forgiven; that's why she loved much. But the one who is forgiven little, loves little.
    Luke 7:47

———

Live in harmony with one another. Do not be proud; instead, associate with the humble. Do not be wise in your own estimation. Do not repay anyone evil for evil. Give careful thought to do what is honorable in everyone's eyes. If possible, as far as it depends on you, live at peace with everyone.
    Romans 12:16–18

Be kind and compassionate to one another, forgiving one another, just as God also forgave you in Christ.

Ephesians 4:32

———

As God's chosen ones, holy and dearly loved, put on compassion, kindness, humility, gentleness, and patience, bearing with one another and forgiving one another if anyone has a grievance against another. Just as the Lord has forgiven you, so you are also to forgive.

Colossians 3:12–13

Dear God, it is easy for me to say that I forgive my friend, but to actually release the resentment from my heart and let it be as if nothing ever happened . . . well I do not have any idea how to do that. Sometimes I feel trapped by the grudges and feelings of hurt that I have chosen to hold on to. I know that the feelings are not only damaging me, but my relationships as well. Please, just as You forgave all my debts and wrongs through Christ, empower me to extend forgiveness to those who have mistreated or hurt me. Amen

Friendship is not usually something that just knocks on your front door and stays forever. It needs to be invited, fostered, cared for, and encouraged. Precious are the friends, neighbors, and colleagues in our lives who faithfully stand by us through joys and sorrows, victories and failures, gains and loss. Find a way today to show the people in your life how much their friendship means to you.

Iron sharpens iron, and one person sharpens another.

   Proverbs 27:17

———

Two are better than one because they have a good reward for their efforts. For if either falls, his companion can lift him up; but pity the one who falls without another to lift him up.

   Ecclesiastes 4:9–10

———

Dear friends, let us love one another, because love is from God, and everyone who loves has been born of God and knows God.

   1 John 4:7

No one has greater love than this: to lay down his life for his friends. You are my friends if you do what I command you. I do not call you servants anymore, because a servant doesn't know what his master is doing. I have called you friends, because I have made known to you everything I have heard from my Father.

John 15:13–15

———

Therefore encourage one another and build each other up as you are already doing.

1 Thessalonians 5:11

Lord Jesus, who called His disciples friends, thank You for demonstrating God's love for us and how best to love one another. Help me to be intentional in my relationships and to grow lifelong friendships. I thank You so much for the friends that You have placed in my life, and I pray that You allow me to be a blessing to them as well. Amen

Goodness is righteousness in action. It is motivated by humility and the desire to bless others. It manifests itself in many different ways within our lives, but is only possible with those who have been filled by the Holy Spirit.

Only goodness and faithful love will pursue me all the days of my life, and I will dwell in the house of the LORD as long as I live.

Psalm 23:6

———

Mankind, he has told each of you what is good and what it is the LORD requires of you: to act justly, to love faithfulness, and to walk humbly with your God.

Micah 6:8

———

Let love be without hypocrisy. Detest evil; cling to what is good.

Romans 12:9

But the fruit of the Spirit is love, joy, peace, patience, kindness, goodness, faithfulness, gentleness, and self-control. The law is not against such things.

Galatians 5:22–23

———

Therefore, as we have opportunity, let us work for the good of all, especially for those who belong to the household of faith.

Galatians 6:10

Father God, thank You for blessing me with the Holy Spirit, and the fruit that He flows through my life. Allow me to be filled with Your goodness so that it pours out of me into all that I do. Open my eyes to the opportunities for me to be a blessing to my friends, family, neighbors, and even to people I do not yet know. Amen

GRACE

Grace is not deserved. It is not needed by the person who has always been reliable, or the child who has never been in trouble. The one who needs your grace is the friend who has cancelled on you four times this week, and now needs your help; the spouse who went on a shopping spree and forgot your birthday; the neighbor who complains about your lawn to others, and now needs help raking. How can you possibly bestow grace on these people? By the grace you have received from the Creator of the universe, you have the power to pass that grace on to others. The greatest gift we will ever receive is grace—the wholly unmerited favor of the Most High. Allow that grace to flow out of you to those who deserve it the least.

The law came along to multiply the trespass. But where sin multiplied, grace multiplied even more.

Romans 5:20

———

For sin will not rule over you, because you are not under the law but under grace.

Romans 6:14

———

Now if by grace, then it is not by works; otherwise grace ceases to be grace.

Romans 11:6

But he said to me, "My grace is sufficient for you, for my power is perfected in weakness." Therefore, I will most gladly boast all the more about my weaknesses, so that Christ's power may reside in me.

    2 Corinthians 12:9

———

For you are saved by grace through faith, and this is not from yourselves; it is God's gift—not from works, so that no one can boast.

    Ephesians 2:8–9

Lord God, thank You for Your riches of grace that have been poured out on me through faith in Christ Jesus. I am left speechless when I think about all the repeated sin in my life that You have wiped clean. I know I do not deserve any of it, and yet Your grace abounds. Help me to show that level of grace to the people in my life. I know that only with Your strength will I be able to repay those who have sinned against me with grace. Amen

No matter how long you have been a Christian, until you get to heaven your sanctification will continue, and you will continue to sin. You are guilty, but Jesus has taken the weight of your guilt and you are found clean before God. Do not continue to live under the weight of what Christ has already died for. Live in the freedom that you have been given.

As far as the east is from the west, so far has he removed our transgressions from us.

Psalm 103:12

———

"Come, let us settle this," says the Lord. "Though your sins are scarlet, they will be as white as snow; though they are crimson red, they will be like wool."

Isaiah 1:18

———

Therefore, there is now no condemnation for those in Christ Jesus, because the law of the Spirit of life in Christ Jesus has set you free from the law of sin and death.

Romans 8:1–2

In him we have redemption through his blood, the forgiveness of our trespasses, according to the riches of his grace.

　　Ephesians 1:7

———

If we confess our sins, he is faithful and righteous to forgive us our sins and to cleanse us from all unrighteousness.

　　1 John 1:9

Father, even though I know that Christ has paid the cost of my sins, I still feel the weight of my guilt holding me down. Lord, remove this guilt from me. Remind me daily that Christ died so that I could live in freedom from condemnation.
Amen

What does happiness look like to you? Is it a good book on the back porch? Or a hike in the mountains with your family? Maybe it's sitting around a campfire laughing with old friends. Though happiness sometimes comes from external circumstances, we experience the most lasting happiness by enjoying our union with Christ.

Therefore my heart is glad and my whole being rejoices; my body also rests securely.

    Psalm 16:9

———

Take delight in the LORD and he will give you your heart's desires.

    Psalm 37:4

———

A joyful heart makes a face cheerful, but a sad heart produces a broken spirit.

    Proverbs 15:13

I know that there is nothing better for them than to rejoice and enjoy the good life.
  Ecclesiastes 3:12

————

Rejoice in the Lord always. I will say it again: Rejoice!
  Philippians 4:4

Lord Jesus, I know that Your desire is for me to be happy. Align the desires of my heart with Your desires, so that I may find full and complete happiness. May my heart be happy and cheerful because I know You. Amen

One of the foundations of a strong friendship is honesty. You cannot have a fruitful relationship without it. Your friends need to know that they can rely on your word and know that you speak truth. It can feel easier to lie, to protect yourself from others by covering yourself with deceit, but this will only lead to heartbreak and destruction. Complete honesty is not possible without the Holy Spirit leading your words and actions. Give Him full control today.

Who is someone who desires life, loving a long life to enjoy what is good? Keep your tongue from evil and your lips from deceitful speech. Turn away from evil and do what is good; seek peace and pursue it.
Psalm 34:12–14

———

Better a poor person who lives with integrity than someone who has deceitful lips and is a fool.
Proverbs 19:1

———

"But let your 'yes' mean 'yes,' and your 'no' mean 'no.' Anything more than this is from the evil one."
Matthew 5:37

Indeed, we are giving careful thought to do what is right, not only before the Lord but also before people.

2 Corinthians 8:21

———

Do not lie to one another, since you have put off the old self with its practices.

Colossians 3:9

Father, lies flow from my lips as easily as air. I change stories, hide feelings, and even gossip about things I know nothing about. I know it is only with Your help that I can remove this sin from my life. Father, guard my tongue that I may no longer speak anything but the truth. Convict me of the deception that I have released, and forgive me for the untrue things I have said. Amen

There is a balance that many people find themselves in, trying to counter-balance their pride by putting themselves down. This is not the same as humility. The key to cultivating true humility isn't to act self-deprecating but to simply not think of oneself much at all. To recognize that it is not about us, but only about God. To give importance to others simply because they are God's creation and deserve to be treated as such.

Sitting down, he called the Twelve and said to them, "If anyone wants to be first, he must be last and servant of all."

　Mark 9:35

———

Live in harmony with one another. Do not be proud; instead, associate with the humble. Do not be wise in your own estimation.

　Romans 12:16

———

Do nothing out of selfish ambition or conceit, but in humility consider others as more important than yourselves.

　Philippians 2:3

*Adopt the same attitude as that of Christ Jesus,
who, existing in the form of God, did not consider
equality with God as something to be exploited.
Instead he emptied himself by assuming the form
of a servant, taking on the likeness of humanity.
And when he had come as a man, he humbled
himself by becoming obedient to the point of
death—even to death on a cross.*

    Philippians 2:5–8

———

*Who among you is wise and understanding? By
his good conduct he should show that his works are
done in the gentleness that comes from wisdom.*

    James 3:13

Lord Jesus, who demonstrated perfect selflessness, please be my vision and my constant focus so that I forget myself completely. It is so easy for me to shift my focus onto myself, and even when I try to correct, I do so by putting myself down. Let me be so consumed by You, that there are no thoughts left for myself. Amen

Our culture is built around the idea of instant gratification, but this is not what God has called us to. The Bible tells us to work hard for the Lord and to strive for our best work in everything that we do. Never allow God's grace to be an excuse for you to sin by not working as hard as you can.

The slacker craves, yet has nothing, but the diligent is fully satisfied.

    Proverbs 13:4

———

The one who is lazy in his work is brother to a vandal.

    Proverbs 18:9

Whatever you do, do it from the heart, as something done for the Lord and not for people, knowing that you will receive the reward of an inheritance from the Lord. You serve the Lord Christ.

  Colossians 3:23–24

———

In fact, when we were with you, this is what we commanded you: "If anyone isn't willing to work, he should not eat."

  2 Thessalonians 3:10

Heavenly God, I know there were times today when I slacked in my responsibilities. I take for granted the rest that You have blessed me with, and I do not use the time You have given me well. Father, help me to see the areas in which I could be doing more. Show me opportunities to work harder for You. Amen

Even surrounded by people it is easy to feel alone. Thanks to social media, and the fast paced modern life has left many of us feeling isolated—but thanks to God's faithful presence and our community of believers, we never have to be alone. Jesus will never leave you or cancel plans. He is always available for you when you need Him.

As he replied, "My presence will go with you, and I will give you rest."

Exodus 33:14

———

The LORD is the one who will go before you. He will be with you; he will not leave you or abandon you. Do not be afraid or discouraged.

Deuteronomy 31:8

———

God provides homes for those who are deserted. He leads out the prisoners to prosperity, but the rebellious live in a scorched land.

Psalm 68:6

He heals the brokenhearted and bandages their wounds.

Psalm 147:3

———

Blessed be the God and Father of our Lord Jesus Christ, the Father of mercies and the God of all comfort. He comforts us in all our affliction, so that we may be able to comfort those who are in any kind of affliction, through the comfort we ourselves receive from God.

2 Corinthians 1:3–4

Father of mercies, please comfort me in times of loneliness so that I may be a comfort to others. Remind me that even in my deepest despair, no matter where I am, You are with me. Thank You for being a constant reminder that I am never alone. Continue to hold me in Your arms, and help me to be a shoulder for others to help them know that I am here for them. Amen

Our highest calling is to love God with all of our heart, our soul, and our mind, and to love our neighbor as ourselves. But what does it mean to love your neighbor as yourself? It is easy to love our friends, but enemies are a whole other story. Only with God's love in our hearts are we able to truly love all people.

But I say to you who listen: Love your enemies, do what is good to those who hate you, bless those who curse you, pray for those who mistreat you.

Luke 6:27–28

———

Love is patient, love is kind. Love does not envy, is not boastful, is not arrogant, is not rude, is not self-seeking, is not irritable, and does not keep a record of wrongs.

1 Corinthians 13:4–5

———

Above all, maintain constant love for one another, since love covers a multitude of sins.

1 Peter 4:8

God's love was revealed among us in this way: God sent his one and only Son into the world so that we might live through him.

1 John 4:9

———

And we have come to know and to believe the love that God has for us. God is love, and the one who remains in love remains in God, and God remains in him.

1 John 4:16

Dear Jesus, there are people in my life that it is hard for me to love. I know that I am still called to love them, but it seems impossible without Your guidance. Instill in my heart the selfless concern and compassion for others that you demonstrated for me. Help me to love people with Your love, and not with what I am capable of on my own. Amen

While other people can only see our actions, God can look at our hearts and see the motives behind what we do. Rather than self-seeking or people-pleasing, we should endeavor to do all things through genuine love for God and others. But that can be harder than it sounds. Use these verses to remind yourself of the importance of what is in your heart.

But the L<small>ORD</small> said to Samuel, "Do not look at his appearance or his stature because I have rejected him. Humans do not see what the L<small>ORD</small> sees, for humans see what is visible, but the L<small>ORD</small> sees the heart."

1 Samuel 16:7

———

All a person's ways seem right to him, but the L<small>ORD</small> weighs hearts.

Proverbs 21:2

———

For am I now trying to persuade people, or God? Or am I striving to please people? If I were still trying to please people, I would not be a servant of Christ.

Galatians 1:10

Do nothing out of selfish ambition or conceit, but in humility consider others as more important than yourselves.

Philippians 2:3

———

Instead, just as we have been approved by God to be entrusted with the gospel, so we speak, not to please people, but rather God, who examines our hearts.

1 Thessalonians 2:4

Lord, please weigh my heart and my reasons for doing the things I do, and reveal to me any motives that don't glorify You. Help me to pull out those motives and change them. Give me a genuine love for the people around me, and move my heart to be so focused on You, that everything I do is glorifying to Your name. Amen

The liveliness of children or the demands of the workplace can rattle your nerves, but take care to avoid making wrong choices or damaging your relationships. Remember the amount of patience that God has given you in your life, and pass it on to the people around you. Not one of us is perfect, and we all need grace and time to find the right path.

The end of a matter is better than its beginning; a patient spirit is better than a proud spirit.

Ecclesiastes 7:8

———

Now if we hope for what we do not see, we eagerly wait for it with patience.

Romans 8:25

———

My dear brothers and sisters, understand this: Everyone should be quick to listen, slow to speak, and slow to anger, for human anger does not accomplish God's righteousness.

James 1:19–20

Therefore, brothers and sisters, be patient until the Lord's coming. See how the farmer waits for the precious fruit of the earth and is patient with it until it receives the early and the late rains. You also must be patient. Strengthen your hearts, because the Lord's coming is near.

James 5:7–8

———

The Lord does not delay his promise, as some understand delay, but is patient with you, not wanting any to perish but all to come to repentance.

2 Peter 3:9

Heavenly Father, You are patient and slow to anger—please help me be still and wait patiently for You. When I start to lose my way and my temper, give me Your calming touch, and help me to take a step back and remember what is really important. Thank You for the strength that You lend to me when I do not have enough myself. Amen

If you are at peace in all of your relationships, it is only a matter of time before conflict will arise. Rather than worry over what has happened in the past or what might happen in the future, be still with the Lord in the peace of the present moment. Be the one to ask for forgiveness, rather than holding on to resentment. Make the first step towards peace.

For I am persuaded that neither death nor life, nor angels nor rulers, nor things present nor things to come, nor powers, nor height nor depth, nor any other created thing will be able to separate us from the love of God that is in Christ Jesus our Lord.
    Romans 8:38–39

———

Peace I leave with you. My peace I give to you. I do not give to you as the world gives. Don't let your heart be troubled or fearful.
    John 14:27

You will keep the mind that is dependent on you in perfect peace, for it is trusting in you.

    Isaiah 26:3

———

And the peace of God, which surpasses all understanding, will guard your hearts and minds in Christ Jesus. Finally brothers and sisters, whatever is true, whatever is honorable, whatever is just, whatever is pure, whatever is lovely, whatever is commendable—if there is any moral excellence and if there is anything praiseworthy—dwell on these things.

    Philippians 4:7–8

Lord Jesus, I feel chaos and conflict in so many areas of my life. It is easy for me to be caught in the mess and forget the perfect peace that You have laid out for me. May Your perfect peace guard my heart and mind as I trust in You. Grant me the humility to seek out peace and be the one to lay down my pride at the feet of conflict, that my relationships may be redeemed. Amen

In the same way that our friendships and relationships with people need communication to be strengthened, so does our relationship with God. He has blessed us with the ability to speak to Him at all times, whenever we need Him. No matter how we come to the Lord, whether to present our requests or to sit silently in His presence, we can trust that He hears us.

"Whenever you pray, you must not be like the hypocrites, because they love to pray standing in the synagogues and on the street corners to be seen by people. . . . But when you pray, go into your private room, shut your door, and pray to your Father who is in secret. And your Father who sees in secret will reward you. When you pray, don't babble like the Gentiles, since they imagine they'll be heard for their many words. . . .

"Therefore, you should pray like this: Our Father in heaven, your name be honored as holy. Your kingdom come. Your will be done on earth as it is in heaven. Give us today our daily bread. And forgive us our debts, as we also have forgiven our debtors. And do not bring us into temptation, but deliver us from the evil one.

"For if you forgive others their offenses, your heavenly Father will forgive you as well. But if you don't forgive others, your Father will not forgive your offenses."

Matthew 6:5–15

If you remain in me and my words remain in you,
ask whatever you want and it will be done for you.
    John 15:7

———

In the same way the Spirit also helps us in our
weakness, because we do not know what to pray for
as we should, but the Spirit himself intercedes for
us with unspoken groanings.
    Romans 8:26

———

Don't worry about anything, but in everything,
through prayer and petition with thanksgiving,
present your requests to God.
    Philippians 4:6

Lord Jesus, just as You taught Your followers how to pray, instill in me a deep desire to seek Your presence. Send reminders into my life of my need to spend time with You. Help me to remember to not only speak in my prayers, but to sit and listen to what You have to tell me. Amen

Pride comes in many shapes and sizes. Arrogance tells us we are better than others, low self-esteem tells us we are worse, and praise makes us feel important, but they are all signs of pride, because they all put the focus on ourselves. Though we may be blessed with wisdom, success, and happy relationships, we can avoid pride by remembering that all good things are ours by the grace of God.

When arrogance comes, disgrace follows, but with humility comes wisdom.

Proverbs 11:2

———

Everyone with a proud heart is detestable to the LORD; be assured, he will not go unpunished.

Proverbs 16:5

———

A person's pride will humble him, but a humble spirit will gain honor.

Proverbs 29:23

Live in harmony with one another. Do not be proud; instead, associate with the humble. Do not be wise in your own estimation.

Romans 12:16

———

For if anyone considers himself to be something when he is nothing, he deceives himself.

Galatians 6:3

Father God, please forgive the ways I puff myself up rather than humble myself under Your loving hand. Help me to forget about myself, and keep my eyes on You. When I fall into a trap of pride, pull me to repentance, that I may not continue to sin against You. I know that any good I am capable of is only because of You. Amen

Friendships can only stand the test of time if both people can be relied upon. A friend who lets you down will not be considered a close friend for very long. But being reliable is not as easy as it sounds. The best way is stay consistent with your word, and when you fail (because you will fail), repent of your wrong doing, and ask for forgiveness.

"*But let your 'yes' mean 'yes,' and your 'no' mean 'no.' Anything more than this is from the evil one.*"
  Matthew 5:37

―――

Whoever is faithful in very little is also faithful in much, and whoever is unrighteous in very little is also unrighteous in much.
  Luke 16:10

What you have heard from me in the presence of many witnesses, commit to faithful men who will be able to teach others also.

2 Timothy 2:2

———

Lᴏʀᴅ, you are my God;
I will exalt you. I will praise your name,
for you have accomplished wonders,
plans formed long ago, with perfect faithfulness.

Isaiah 25:1

Father, help me to stop making false promises where I cannot follow through. I want to be a reliable friend, but I know that I cannot do that on my own. I need Your strength. Thank You for being my example of what it means to be reliable. You are always there for me, and I know that with Your power behind me, I will be able to be reliable.

Sacrifice is painful. It is the offering up of something important for a higher purpose. It is only possible when you have full confidence in that higher purpose. As Christians, we know that we are called to sacrifice every part of our lives for the higher purpose of God's will. Through Him we know that every sacrifice is worth it.

*Then Abraham reached out and took the knife to slaughter his son. But the angel of the L*ORD *called to him from heaven and said, "Abraham, Abraham!" He replied, "Here I am."*

Then he said, "Do not lay a hand on the boy or do anything to him. For now I know that you fear God, since you have not withheld your only son from me."

Genesis 22:10–12

———

But God proves his own love for us in that while we were still sinners, Christ died for us.

Romans 5:8

"This is my command: Love one another as I have loved you. No one has greater love than this: to lay down his life for his friends. You are my friends if you do what I command you."
   John 15:12–14

———

Don't neglect to do what is good and to share, for God is pleased with such sacrifices.
   Hebrews 13:16

Christ Jesus, You have sacrificed more than I could ever imagine, all to take my place in death. I know that You have called me to the same level of sacrifice, but I am afraid. I am afraid that when the time comes I will not be able to stand up as Abraham did and be willing to give up everything for You. Grant me courage in my walk. Hold my focus on what is truly important so that I am not distracted by anything else. Help me to hold everything in my life in an open palm, knowing that it all ultimately belongs to You. Amen

It is not when you are prepared that your true character shines; it is when the unexpected happens. When you find out a friend lied to you, when you get cut off in traffic; when your child starts biting, that is when you see if your walls have the strength to hold together your responses in a way that is pleasing to God. It is in the unexpected that your self-control has a chance to shine. Think about how you have responded in situations that you were unprepared for recently. Are you proud of the result, or with more time would you have responded differently? Use these verses to strengthen your self-control, so that when the expected opportunities arise, you allow the Holy Spirit to respond through you.

A person who does not control his temper is like a city whose wall is broken down.

    Proverbs 25:28

———

No temptation has come upon you except what is common to humanity. But God is faithful; he will not allow you to be tempted beyond what you are able, but with the temptation he will also provide a way out so that you may be able to bear it.

    1 Corinthians 10:13

*Finally brothers and sisters, whatever is
true, whatever is honorable, whatever is just,
whatever is pure, whatever is lovely, whatever is
commendable—if there is any moral excellence and
if there is anything praiseworthy—dwell on these
things.*

Philippians 4:8

———

*Be sober-minded, be alert. Your adversary the devil
is prowling around like a roaring lion, looking for
anyone he can devour.*

1 Peter 5:8

Father, at times I feel as if I lose myself to my reactions. I let the flow of my emotions control my decisions, rather than having them rooted in You. God, control my heart. Help me to think through my actions and reactions. Let me not be swept up in a moment, but be rooted so firmly in Scripture, that no matter what comes my way I am as steady as Your Word. Amen

TRUST

Trust is not an easy thing to give away. Everyone has had a time when their trust has been given to a friend, only to be betrayed. But God is not a fallible human. To trust the Lord is to believe what He has said about Himself: He is good, faithful, and sovereign. He is always worthy and deserving of our trust.

The person who trusts in the LORD, whose confidence indeed is the LORD, is blessed. He will be like a tree planted by water: it sends its roots out toward a stream, it doesn't fear when heat comes, and its foliage remains green. It will not worry in a year of drought or cease producing fruit.

Jeremiah 17:7–8

————

Wait for the LORD; be strong, and let your heart be courageous. Wait for the LORD.

Psalm 27:14

————

And my God will supply all your needs according to his riches in glory in Christ Jesus.

Philippians 4:19

I will be with you when you pass through the waters, and when you pass through the rivers, they will not overwhelm you. You will not be scorched when you walk through the fire, and the flame will not burn you.
    Isaiah 43:2

———

This is the confidence we have before him: If we ask anything according to his will, he hears us.
    1 John 5:14

Dear God, thank You that all things work together for the good of those who love You and are called according to Your purpose. Amen

Worry is false and useless fear—it's imagining and anticipating what might happen but probably won't. What can you change by worrying about it? Nothing. What can you fix by thinking about everything that could go wrong? Nothing. Instead, spend your time focused on today. On what you can do, on what you know to be truth, and leave the rest to God.

Therefore I tell you: Don't worry about your life, what you will eat or what you will drink; or about your body, what you will wear. Isn't life more than food and the body more than clothing? Consider the birds of the sky: They don't sow or reap or gather into barns, yet your heavenly Father feeds them. Aren't you worth more than they? Can any of you add one moment to his life-span by worrying?

Matthew 6:25–27

———

The Lord answered her, "Martha, Martha, you are worried and upset about many things, but one thing is necessary. Mary has made the right choice, and it will not be taken away from her."

Luke 10:41–42

*We know that all things work together for the good
of those who love God, who are called according to
his purpose.*

    Romans 8:28

—————

*Don't worry about anything, but in everything,
through prayer and petition with thanksgiving,
present your requests to God. And the peace of God,
which surpasses all understanding, will guard your
hearts and minds in Christ Jesus.*

    Philippians 4:6–7

Lord Jesus, I am often worried about many things. I worry about tomorrow, about my family, about what friends are really thinking, about health, about clothes, about money, and about countless other meaningless things. Jesus, I know that my worry will do nothing, but the thoughts are rooted in my mind, and I know I cannot remove them without Your help. Remind me of Your provision. Show me ways to let go of my worry. Please grant me a heart like Mary, who rested at Your feet. Amen

VERSE INDEX